For Audrey & Owen—
You are the Coolest!
Love, Mom

Published in the United States
by Xist Publishing
www.xistpublishing.com
PO Box 61593 Irvine, CA 92602

Text Copyright © 2020 by Calee M. Lee
Illustration Copyright © 2020 by Brenda Ponnay
All rights reserved
No portion of this book may be reproduced without express permission of the publisher
First Edition

Hardcover ISBN: 978-1-5324-1558-6
Paperback ISBN: 978-1-5324-1557-9
eISBN: 978-1-5324-1556-2

Download a free eBook copy of this book using this QR code.*

or at http://xist.pub/06c9b

* Limited time only
Your name and a valid email address are required to download.
Must be redeemed by persons over 13

You are the Coolest

Positive Puns for Kids

written by Calee M. Lee
illustrated by Brenda Ponnay

Taco 'bout an amazing kid...

It will be a piece of cake!

Stay sharp!

You've turtle-y got this!

I see grape-ness in you!

You are purr-fect to me.

prrrrrr....

Do your zest!

It sure is ice to see you!

I'm snow sorry,

but you will get through this.

You are Dino-mite!

Bee amazing!

You are one cute tea!

You are berry special!

www.ingramcontent.com/pod-product-compliance
Lightning Source LLC
LaVergne TN
LVHW070950070426
835507LV00030B/3474